RADIOAPOCRYPHA

*THE JOURNAL* CHARLES B. WHEELER POETRY PRIZE

# RADIOAPOCRYPHA

## BK FISCHER

MAD CREEK BOOKS, AN IMPRINT OF
THE OHIO STATE UNIVERSITY PRESS • COLUMBUS

Copyright © 2018 by The Ohio State University.
All rights reserved.
Mad Creek Books, an imprint of The Ohio State University Press.

Library of Congress Cataloging-in-Publication Data
Names: Fischer, B. K., author.
Title: Radioapocrypha / B. K. Fischer.
Description: Columbus : Mad Creek Books, an imprint of The Ohio State University
    Press, [2018] | Includes bibliographical references. | "Winner of the 2017 The
    Ohio State University Press/"The Journal" Charles B. Wheeler Poetry Prize"
Identifiers: LCCN 2017041986 | ISBN 9780814254646 (pbk. ; alk. paper) | ISBN
    0814254640 (pbk. ; alk. paper)
Classification: LCC PS3606.I764 R33 2018 | DDC 813/.6—dc23
LC record available at https://lccn.loc.gov/2017041986

Cover design by Laurence J. Nozik
Text design by Juliet Williams
Type set in Adobe Palatino and Futura

♾ The paper used in this publication meets the minimum requirements of the
American National Standard for Information Sciences—Permanence of Paper for
Printed Library Materials. ANSI Z39.48-1992.

9  8  7  6  5  4  3  2  1

*for James, setting out*

# CONTENTS

This is she.

Speaking.




Sorry, I didn't mean to
    hang up on you, you
caught me off guard—
    he was—          I wasn't—
all of that happened
    in another life, none
of it matters now.

# ENUNCIATION

Damnation was a staple of the sophomore curriculum.
      Look under your chairs: a masking-tape X
marks the elect, salvation for the few, the popular.

      Thus ended the lesson on Calvinism and we turned
to *The Crucible,* cut third period as often as possible
      and tromped through the woods to Lucky's Deli

for Lucky Strikes. I shouldn't be telling you any of this.
      *Can you enter your mother's womb a second time?*
I have no idea where he is, maybe out West? Iceland?

      New Zealand? dead? I don't want to know. I have
kids of my own now, middle-schoolers, a girl and a boy,
      a garden. It's not that I don't remember, I remember

every word and I feel sorry for her, the girl I was—
      bruised, observant, adoring. They told us the world
would end and it didn't. They told us we'd die, then we

      didn't. Callahan sat us down to settle the score. He
was a master of sarcasm, the master of ceremonies. He was
      a lover and a healer. He was a real son of a bitch.

## OUR LADY OF THE SUBDIVISION

I was the prodigal returning to the split level
       in disgrace, retreating to my room
with its baby-blue shag and locking the door
       anyone over the age of three could jimmy
with a bobby pin. I slept off the stray clichés—
       slunk home, licked wounds, hung tail—
tried to forget about the inpatient clinic where
       even the lauded daughter is served up
the same pills in a soufflé cup. The sort of town
       where neighbors cluck about over-
reach: valedictoriana and an El Dorado
       parked next to a Secret Service vehicle
overnight, forsythia and a plastic fawn with
       a planter in its back, a Jeep on blocks,
hoses coiled under crepe myrtles, gas grills,
       service revolver in a drawer by the bed.

Through the girl-curtains, I saw Mrs. C. midway
       through her lunchtime walk around
each cul-de-sac—Autumnwood, Winterhaven,
       Summerhill—taking the "over" off
achiever: overboard, overdone, overwrought,
       because overnight I was too big for my
britches, a good girl in November and then not,
       drawstring cinched tighter by the turn
of the year. New Year's at a propane hearth.

       I left college without finishing the first term,
went home to my parents and my quadriplegic
       betta fish, which senior year had contracted
some fungus that ate away its azure fins but
       did not kill it. It scooched to the surface
for food, twitched its pinky-finger body. I wanted
       to flush it, but my mother took on its care
when I went to school. I came home, resumed my
       duties—pinched flakes, swabbed the bowl.

# (TEACHER)

It really stinks in here—you guys should leave the doors open once in a while, think about bringing in some plants. Nice guitar. Move that lamp out from under the bucket or you're going to burn the place down. That or a half-dead oak will drop a limb on this roof with the heft of a girder. Let's get a few things straight. *No bullying, no blackmail.* Don't wear words on your clothes unless it's a band. You can drop the "Mr." when we're not at school. *I don't come to abolish but to complete.* You've got to stop listening to this pop shit. I'll tell you what, *let's cross over to the other side of the lake*: say it don't spray it, root for the underdog, give to anyone who asks. Lurk in the upstairs hall of an unkempt raised ranch, where people live after they've given up on making living look cute, when they've stopped clearing piles off the coffee table or putting the dishes back in the cabinet. Where they move from bed to bathroom, leaving the washcloth on the edge of the tub. *Moth and rust destroy.* You're the sonic youth of a daydream nation. *Reach out and touch faith.*

# PARABLE OF THE MOWER

One airless August afternoon, half a dozen kids
got hired for $3 an hour to pass out a thousand flyers
for the heating and cooling company owned by one

of their dads, covering a neighborhood with streets
named for poets: Keats, Spenser, Sidney, Pope.
Municipal mowers droned from the drainage sloughs

between the houses and ball fields, scattering
grass clippings as they crossed the medians
and idled at the curbs. The only girl in the group

noticed that most of the driveways she climbed
to tuck the rolled-up flyer in the storm door
had oil spots in the shape of horses. On one,

a bloodied mouse was caught under a piece
of green tinsel—when it lifted off the corpse
she saw that it was a swarm of emerald flies.

# OUR LADY OF WALGREENS

I stopped going out much after I overheard,
        from the bathroom stall in the bowling alley,
*Maren Manning got knocked up but it was*
        *an alien so she threw it in the dumpster.*

It was a Tuesday, just after midnight—I went
        to the pharmacy in flannel, waited while
the tech counted out 45 fluoxetine. I was trying
        to lay off the Xanax and listen to my mother
about chamomile and prayer but I itched and
        chewed a pack of Big Red one stick after
another, tongue burning with cinnamon, only
        Pantene and Secret Solid to soothe me.
I was the lone customer at that hour but hid
        in cosmetics, where I uncapped a lipstick,
tested Plum Liquor on the back of my hand.

        When I looked up, there he was, bending
toward shampoo. Callahan, at 33, looked like

        he'd barely started to shave, glossy curls
longish but not quite a mullet. I picked up
        a pack of emery boards, put it back on
the hook. There were three sizes of nail clippers.

        I closed my eyes and saw it again—red
smear, retinal Rorschach of my ailing December,
        the ache in my gut, flush of sweat rising
to my neck. I don't think I said a word to him
        that night, just managed a nod when he said

*I heard you were home, taking a break from college.*
        *I'm a night owl myself.* I bolted—riveted
to the spot, fleeing the scene—jumped when
        I hit the cold air of the parking lot and
saw his mom in the passenger seat of his Nissan,
        riffling through her wallet for a card.

## (KIDDIE POOL)

Don't take things so personally, Parker. Your anger is fed by snow-melt and advertising. The insurgency began and you were too busy feeling sorry for your latchkey self to fix your own goddamn snack. On August 11, 1985, a small toxic cloud escaped from a Union Carbide plant in Institute, West Virginia, which officials denied contained methyl isocyanate, the chemical that had escaped from another Union Carbide plant and killed 2,000 people in Bhopal, India, the previous December. I despise principals but I got this job to get my mother out of there. You can come in, Jordan Cisco, I don't bite. *If the world hates you, keep in mind that it hated me first.* Listen up. When you leave here tonight, walk to the top of Maytime Drive—a mother will run screaming from a split-level, a child limp in her arms. A bigger child will run after her saying they were just playing. She was pouring water from scoops into the plastic mill wheel and her sister was pretending to sleep. She told her to. The mother will collapse on the lawn with the child. Go to her. Tell her the bigger child is right: she is only sleeping. Tell her to give the child a sippy cup.

# OUR LADY OF CINDERBLOCK

You've seen the made-for-TV movie: a fling
          on a fall weekend with a fencer, not one
of the frat boys but still too cool for me—
          upperclassman, upper class. I was
beer-sloshed in the whiplash of first failure,
          a test that afternoon I couldn't finish,
questions that swerved from comprehension,
          blank page handed to the morbid TA.

I sat on a stoop in unseasonable warmth, studied
          his calves and triceps while he stood near
the keg. I wanted to see if I could do it, deliberate,
          not the way it was with boyfriends,
the patient fumbling, the hapless consent, but zero
          to flesh in a single hour, from a stranger to
hands in hair, shoulders, breath. Turns out I could.

          At Thanksgiving I was late. I chewed
the string of my hooded sweatshirt on the train back
          to campus. Finals week I started to shake—
night sweats, vertigo. I slept. I stopped going
          to the dining hall or the lounge on my floor.
Three or four days, no more, watching the light
          change the color of the cinderblock wall
from almond to almost rose to gold, a pocked wall
          where I made out a haloed matron's face.
I lay there on the bed rolling a piece of putty
          between my fingers, pushing my foot where
the corner of the poster kept coming up. Then

there was pain and I lay on the floor. I tried
to spell *gelatin, sacrilege, hemorrhage,* wondered
        if it had a head and a tail. My roommate's
lime-green water bottle had rolled under the bed
        and I thought she'd be happy I found it.
She was on the swim team. When she came back
        from weight training she thought I'd tried
to kill myself, climbed over the bed to avoid
        the puddle and get the phone. Campus
EMS seemed eager to have something to do.

# OUR LADY OF THE GARAGE BAND

Parker lived behind me; our backyards touched.
        Before we knew we were a boy and a girl,
we hopped the fence both ways, invented realms,
        aquatic and arboreal labyrinths to lay
our scarabs in. He was a few months younger
        but a year behind in school, so when I
came home that fall he was a senior vibrating
        at the point of extinction, hanging out
in his parents' detached garage with the rest:
        Levi, Jake, Oscar, Danny, Jordan Cisco.

That was the actual band. The others came
        and went, but they were there—Jeff,
Mike T., Mike R., Zack, Greg, Lorenzo.
        I don't remember any of them having
steady girlfriends, but a few loner girls from
        the sophomore class called themselves
groupies—Rachelle, Stacy, a blond named Kim.

        Nothing had changed. Same lion-shaped
oil stain they called Neruda, ping-pong table,
        TV, drum set, amps, gum wrappers,
Cheetos, extension cords, Little Debbies,
        guitar picks. Nail points poking through
the roof. Parker flopped on an orange couch
        with rattan arms he jabbed with a pencil,
his acned chin on a pink pillow that seemed
        breaded and fried in the fur of a black lab.
*Geraldo Rivera. M\*A\*S\*H. Goonies* on VHS.

        Mrs. C. was always around—she bought
or sold Amway, I can't remember which, to or
        from Parker's mom—and when she backed
out of the driveway they turned up the speakers
        so the bass became seismic in the floor,

harmonic squeals that stripped the rust off
      the center beam and stung the sinuses.
I was sure the screaming would break a face
      or pop a vein, but what did I know,
watching them swish their greasy hair around
      then tap a ditty rhythm on a trash-can rim.

Lorenzo flexed his double-jointed thumbs.
      Mike R. and Zack liked each other and
everyone knew it but no one said anything,
      just kept on trying to write a song that
would stop sounding like "Love in an Elevator."

# (LITMUS)

You think you can hold a piece of pH paper up to a person and tell if a taste of him will burn the tongue? Dilute your fear. A dye extracted from lichen: blue turns red in the presence of an acid; red turns blue in the presence of an alkali. Boys of the border states, you seem to forget we're south of the Mason-Dixon in a swamp that would have seceded if Lincoln hadn't held it under martial law. Draw a sip of the sample into the paper and see. No, I don't have a perm. What the hell is wrong with you, Jordan—we don't go around touching people's hair like it's a petting zoo. I've dined with drummers against my better judgment. I've tried to titrate this poison one drop at a time. I've tested eighty drams of antidote. We need a deluge. Nobody believes me, but Antron McCray, Kevin Richardson, Yusef Salaam, Raymond Santana, and Korey Wise, held tonight in the 20th precinct in Manhattan, are innocent. We need a water-soluble mixture. We need the rate of forward reaction to exceed the rate of reverse reaction. In a state of equilibrium, reactants and products come to rest in concentrations that have no further tendency to change. No further tendency to change with time. Equilibrium is not peace.

## OUR LADY OF THE HAIR CUTTERY

If you put an ear-piercing gun on the dash
        in the first act, it's going to go off
in the car. For the record I only have two
        additional holes in myself besides
the ones I was born with—I missed out
        on pierced noses and navels, tats.
I was Keds, leggings, over-sized cable knits,
        Big Hair up-bangs, which was harder
on some of us than others—mousy fine wisps

        meant a curling iron crusted with hair
spray and back-combed roots teased stiff
        with gum arabic and damage, submission
to the polymer burn of the perm—all for a fan
        rising from the forehead a few years
past Farrah Faucet but indebted
        to the shoulder-padded ethic of gel.

Walk-ins only—I put my name on the pad,
        studied the bale of cotton batting used
to wrap the face, scissors and combs in blue
        cylinders of disinfectant, salon products,
pomades. Senior stylist Candi and a scarlet A.

        Donna Callahan was the last woman
in America to sit under a globe dryer paging
        through *People.* If she recognized me
when I sat down in the chair and was lurched
        up three pumps, gowned and clipped
with a paper bib, she didn't say so or smile.

        Candi cleared her throat. Trim up
the split ends, hon? No, I said, do a big chop.
        Bob, pixie, wedge, I don't care what
you call it. Take it off. Take it up to my ears.

## GARAGE GOSPEL

After they all left

he unwrapped the fruit from the pages of the A&P circular—super-
    saver Saturday, three for one

peaches—laid them on the ping-pong table

*every modeled form every creature exists in and with each other will dis-*
    *solve again into their own proper root*

put his hand on the nape of my neck, my throat

*disturbing confusion then occurred in the whole body*

he laughed, held my bangs back from my forehead

*chain of forgetfulness*

parted my mouth with a fingertip

*the first form is darkness the second is desire*

fingertip across the lip

you're ok with this?

*not laying down any other rule or law*

took his two arms in my two hands

hand on the small of my back

*more than all other women*

hand stays there

you're sure you're ok?

steps back to unzip his fly

*foolish wisdom of the flesh*

stumbles with the cuffs

*no such thing as sin*

thumb pressed into the navel, thumb

*did he, then, speak with a woman in private without our knowing*

panty elastic

*who are you then for your part to reject*

palm flat on the last bones of the spine

*stones will shout out*

## OUR LADY OF THE BAY

An April mist gave way to overcast glare
        that made me wish for sunglasses,
for respite from the ranks of disaffected geeks,
        from my mother, who took me out to lunch
to talk about what I was going to do after my
        "medical leave." We sat on a bench
at the Edgewater dock, watched the watermen
        run their trotlines, pull up baits spaced
at six-foot intervals, netting the number ones
        and leaving the sooks. My mother never

talked very much. She pointed out a cormorant.
        Her father had been a crabber for two
decades after retiring from DuPont, half local,
        half chicken-necker. (Tourists bait
with chicken necks; natives use bull lips and
        razor clams, or eel.) A diesel workboat
pulled in and sputtered beside the pilings.

        She stood up, shielded her eyes, so I knew
I'd dodged another attempt: I'm supposed
        to be _____, so you can feel _____
about this. Waft of diesel. My mother's hand,
        held to her forehead, looking at the bay.
Lay your shoulders back, Maren. She was right,

        my shoulders hinged badly in their sockets.
I made an awkward, birdlike shape in space.

## (HOMEOPATH)

Parker, please sit down. When you are waiting at a railroad crossing and a freight goes by, boxcar after boxcar, tanker after tanker—milk, oil, milk, oil—when you are sitting there hating your life and tanning one arm, no one is watching. A filament clinks in a burned-out light bulb. Jordan, try to love a little of what you hate. A sip of venom. In 1983, a 17-year-old boy took a dare and disappeared off the ledge of Swingle's, the deepest quarry in Quincy, Massachusetts. The mayor had it filled in. Rewind that: *let's put our heads together and start a new country up.* Mercy, not justice. Once a man came to me with hands he had tried to burn off. He tried to burn them off after he hurt his wife, but he couldn't do it, stopped after the first blisters. Another time, a woman said she'd offer me an hour with her daughters for a sum, to make rent. Let me put my hands on you, and your fever will break.

# OUR LADY OF 80s PUNK

The adrenal beat put Parker in a meditative state,
     legs over the arms of the couch, lips
pooching in and out. I didn't understand
     the music—I was a headache-prone
goody-goody tuning my radio prudishly to
     the Fine Young Cannibals, awful
Paula Abdul, Tone Lōc, Bad English, Milli
     Vanilli, The Bangles, Tears for Fears,
Bette Midler's "Wings" so ubiquitous that year
     Danny crushed something whenever he
heard it. Mike R. had his Madonna, like a prayer.

     What they were after, what they sought—
they wanted acceleration and shriek, raw
     cochlea and amphetamine strike, restive
with their drumsticks and steel cylinders from
     some junk heap scavenged when they were
*looking for a man with a focus and a temper,* keyed up
     bastards of young: *we are the sons of no one.*

Callahan nodded. He took up their tattered
     cassettes, rewound them with an eraser,
scrawled Hüsker Dü in chalk on the floor
     and ripped a pillowcase into white strips
to wave in woe and surrender. Levi never
     blinked. He was the bassist and he kept
everything in his head, I could tell. Danny
     was the only one who could sing on key—
Parker couldn't carry Happy Birthday—though
     Oscar on keyboard had some serious piano
lessons behind him. Jordan Cisco on drums.

     Callahan came around at dusk with records
and advice, often donuts, always an anecdote or two
     to mock the other teachers and the cliques,
and most days he picked up a guitar. Those hands.

Donna Callahan used to wear her son's
old concert T-shirts to her Jazzercise class,
            the ones that didn't fit him since he'd lost
so much weight. It was hard to imagine him
            a husky kid, fat teen, slim as he was then
in his aviator jacket and black jeans. None

            of us could stop looking at him, none
of us understood we had stepped into the roil
            of woe and surrender. Parker thought
he did—*I've been waiting for a guide to come
            and take me by the hand*—strumming
alongside him, imitating his gestures,
            his gait, gathering momentum, heat,
while *the spirit of a new sensation took hold.*

# (PREDESTINATION)

Is rockslide. Is tabletop. Is wind farm. Is dry run. Is dry clean only.
Is water tower. Is shoplift. Is walkout. Is walkout basement. Is cell. Is
cell sample from the tongue. Is sine curve. Is synecdoche. Is shame.
Is a shame. Is a rabbit's foot. Is ground fault. Is steak knife. Is alka-
line. Is merchandise. Is mullet. Is cleft palate. Is gifted and talented.
Is sunscreen. Is screen door. Is industrial solvent. Is gasoline splashed
through a funnel. Is carpenter ants. Is impulse buy. Is oil spill. Is nod-
ding off. Is hard line. Is hard drive. Is die hard. Is nervous wreck. Is
wreck. Is walking away from the wreck. Is walking away from the
wreck unharmed.

## OUR LADY OF THE BACHELOR PAD

Oh he totally had a weird thing going on
       with his mother, but what did we know.
We didn't even think it was odd he wanted to
       spend so much time with a bunch of kids,
because we didn't think we were kids, we thought
       we were going to rule the world with chords
and clairvoyant singles, hot mercy and radical love.
       His dad had left when he was six, moved
to Vancouver. His mom was a speech therapist
       working in the district part-time. I can see

where people got the wrong idea, but in truth
       all we could see was his face—in daylight
and dream, in rearview or over the hood, outside
       any pane. Tuesday nights he tutored me

at his place, a condo with a new-car smell.
       His mom stopped by with dinners in Pyrex,
the comforter that had been too big to fit
       in his washing machine, Ralph Lauren
navy plaid. That print still reminds me of sex,
       of getting out of his shower, collapsing
at his feet with my wet hair while he traced
       letters one by one on the back of my
neck, repeating any figure if I didn't catch
       the code. Then there were long Sundays
when I said I was shopping with friends, hours
       with nothing but our bodies, insensible

to time or space outside the square of his bed
        and the square of light inside that square,
until I thought of school or the world and pulled
        away, scooted up the pillows and away
from his mouth, worried he'd be grossed out
        because I had that just-in-case pantiliner
down there all day, coffee dregs, but he said,
        you taste like moss and citrus and bay.
I wanted to return it, to match his mouth with
        mouth and his word with word, buried
my face in his coiled hair, ashen black, like
        chalk, like blackboard erasers, dusty felt.

## (HALF LIFE)

Listen, you're making this harder than it is—it's the amount of time required for a quantity to fall to half its value as measured at the beginning. Half, then half of that. Don't get thrown off by this idea of exponential decay, we're talking about something going down, losing potency, not rising to a higher power. It's the time required probabilistically for half of the unstable radioactive atoms in a sample to undergo radioactive decay. I shouldn't have said that. Look at me. Think of an aspirin. *Lilies never spin or weave.* You are more beautiful than you know. *I'm your messiah and you're the reason why.* My dad's in Winnipeg now, or he was. Measure the amount of drug in the plasma at intervals. Water has a half life of about nine to ten days; cesium, one to four months. Think of a teaspoon of salt dissolving in a glass, then a gallon, then a bay. It never disappears.

## PARABLE OF THE SLUT

Tina drove with one hand, palming the wheel
to protect her polish, thinking about the word
someone had Sharpied on her locker, the looseness

of the capital S, the rumor that the quiet Lebanese
girl across from her in home ec was the victim
of a supernatural impregnation. Virtue intact,

the girl sat between her parents at the D.A.R.E.
assembly. Unlike herself, she thought, who
threw out flyers about things like that, who

took the career test and scored high for nurse
and insurance underwriter. She tried touching
pinkie nails together at the red light—still tacky.

## (MOJO)

Mooning is racist since it presumes a white ass. Take a look at your own sorry behinds: eight white, two black, two brown. Suburbia homogenizes its milk. That word you keep using, do you even know what it means? *Mojo,* opposite of jinx—amulet fetish mascot periapt charm—from *moco,* Gullah for witchcraft. None of you have any idea what I'm talking about. All right. Zip up your Members Only jackets and go down to the old graveyard in the swamp in South River. They're about to bulldoze it to build more of those rabbit-hutch one-, two-, and three-bedroom units with covered parking spots. When you find it, go around the fence and walk into the muck. You'll feel the ghosts right away—they'll force your head down, like a sneeze, just to let you know they're there. Look around and pick up some of the grave goods, half buried in mud, half covered in pond water, three soggy states after after-the-rain—moldy calico dolls, snuff pouches, calfskin hoods. Read the names of boys buried with their killed clocks. Earwigs will skitter out. None of you are ready for this. Go get the shit scared out of you, then come back. February never did endure its dormancy.

# OUR LADY OF THE ACCESS ROAD

He pulled off the I-95 bypass, tires crunching
       to a halt on the gravel shoulder, came around
to offer me a hand over the guardrail. In a week
       the flank of trees had greened, the face

of the Madonna blurred in birches in the stretch
       between exits. He sent me up the slope,
went back to the car for a blanket, and I stepped
       into the long grass. When I turned I saw

him see me. You don't understand. I saw the scene
       he saw me in, a painted-over photograph
with my body—dark figure—in the unpainted gap
       of it, reversal of vision and painted foliage,

feathers, intricate wildflowers in pimento reds,
       peacock aquas, indigos in the margins.
I saw the fleshy foliage in which he found me,
       slouching into my shoulders, hair falling

along my jaw, mirrored shades, mere suggestion
       of a mouth. Tall fescue, torn piece of taffeta
on a thornbush. He gave it to my mind, the vista,
       as the devil gave him the cities from the hill.

## (INSOMNIA)

Sweet Maren, relent. You are naked because you peeled your damp tank top over your head as you slept. You were clench-jawed and calling out about the Iron Curtain and the iron lung, voodoo, Virginia Woolf, Watergate, the last man standing in a field of wheat. You're here, with me, in the bedroom. Sit up and see by moonlight—there's the picture on the wall, the shape of the fruit, the shaded side of the bowl. Find your spot here on my chest, your damp ear, damp tendril. A carpet will slip on its carpet pad. *Prophesies will cease, tongues will be stilled, knowledge will pass away. Only love remains.* You don't need to get up again for a drink of water. You don't need to pee. You don't need to put your knee on the vanity to get a closer look at your imperfections. Believe me. The perfect is the enemy of the good.

## OUR LADY OF THE QUARRY

We met the others on Wolf Pit Road,
      scrabbled up dirt bike trails to a place
where the chain-link fence was ripped back
      to make a portal. The gash in the hill
surprised us every time, the exposed strata,
      gravel giving way—an open mine for
aggregate or slate, gabbro or riprap. Probably
      none of those things, probably sand,

clay-tinted sand we knew by taste, touch—
      in gullies, in trucks along the Patuxent
rail bed, grit in their wake, pebbles hailing
      the windshield. Nothing struck us
as odd about acres of pine cleared for tons
      of sand-under-soil, far from the shore,
a 12-foot berm to muffle sound, block
      view. *Sitting in a sand pit, life is*
*a short trip, the music's for the sad man.*

      He could have been any smart boy
from an Appalachian town with a library,
      Callahan, caller from a narrow forest.
We followed him well enough by half moon,
      heavy equipment long gone, first
sign of groundwater seeping at our feet.

      When we reached the top we could
see Waugh Chapel substation—titan arms
      and galactic ropes, converter cables
shunting voltage high to low. Once, he said,
      he saw a cave under the northern hill
of Bezetha; another time, a substation disguised
      as a ranch-style house with lawn, shrubs,
driveway. As he spoke he started to conduct

radioactive heat, like insulator coils
glowing red then blue, the lightning arresters
    at the compass points throwing ionic
circuits in long arcs over his head. Parker

    leapt to his feet, shouted that he'd build
a dunking booth for him and Abraham
    Lincoln at the Anne Arundel County Fair.

When I dared look up again, I saw his mother
    walking along the rim, picking up trash.

## PARABLE OF THE CHEERLEADER

Kelly needed more stuff that looked good on her
college application so she volunteered to pair up
with a kid in special ed through a program called

Buddies, helped him with his homework, smiled
when she saw him at his locker. She got used to
his acne and arcana, copied his lists from Slavic myth

in her bubbly handwriting, showed him how to
fold a dollar bill into a ring. Her jackass boyfriend
dumped her right before prom so she asked the kid—

talked to his mom, pinned his boutonniere, tugged
the jacket of his rented tux straight on his scoliotic
shoulders. He gave her a geode and a runic charm.

At the dance she ditched him for a bit, hung out in
the ladies' room smoking a joint and reapplying
lipstick with her friends, but mostly she was nice.

## OUR LADY OF SAFEWAY

Donna Callahan remembers how they tried
       to arrest her when she was young, how
her fiancé swallowed his pride and pulled her
       away from the edge of the dusty pit.
She wears her kelly-green polo shirt tucked
       into belted jeans, keeps her hair neat
in a tight perm, works the boosters booth
       at halftime and stocks the napkins.

Donna Callahan reaches for the half gallon
       in the back of the case, for Yoplait
and Fluffernutter, for Kix, Trix, Chex Mix,
       Kleenex, Carmex, Tex-Mex, samples
by the deli bell: cubed cheese on toothpicks.

       Worried, she calls over to her son—
the wine is about to run out (*that is no concern*
       *of mine*) and she gives him a look, so
he wills the best vintage into a foil pouch with
       a spigot (*now draw some off*), where it
will never spoil, then strides through automatic
       doors without treading on the mat.

## (SHEPHERD)

Don't be a sheep, Parker. We'll make do without electrocuting devices. Escape the piped-in soundtrack in the waiting room, the Musak in the supermarket. The problem with your scenario is the expectation of safety, when it is only an illusion, a reasonable hypothesis based on outcomes in the past. I'm not going to leave you out there by yourself, but please bring a compass. We are not illegitimate. *Take the plank out of your own eye.* Try another chord—you keep falling into the theme from *Top Gun.* How am I going to get this through to you clowns? I'm in the milk and the milk's in me? If you get on a seesaw—the saint goes up, the sinner goes down, the holy goes up, the profane comes down—if you stay on the teeter-tottcr, suuner or later the other guy's going to hop off and let you hit the ground with a hell of a cherry bomb. Ever watch a pelican take off? That's how they figured out the DC-10. If a girl is wearing cut-off shorts with peace signs on her butt cheeks, make friends with her.

## OUR LADY OF MARSHALLS

I was never first to him. No one was.
       He told us everything, explained
everything, revealed nothing, spoke
       in jingles and riddles, *figs*
*from thistles, mint and dill and cumin,*
       *two sparrows sold for a penny.*
*Neither moth nor rust. Does this shock you?*
       *Quit complaining among yourselves.*

I fretted away hours while I waited
       for him to finish work and pick me up,
drive to the lake—circled the clearance rack
       from small to XXL, tried on pre-ripped
jeans, fringed viscose halter tops, rhinestone-
       studded ballet flats, browsed the brocade
carry-ons, beds in bags, polyester lingerie,
       a kettle with a missing lid for cheap.

I was admitted to the fitting room with
       a meaningless plastic tag—four—
disrobed in a stall with discarded garments
       on every hook, smell of solvents
and somebody's perfume—pardon us,

       we forgot to remove the inventory-
control label from your purchase, *thief*—
       those fierce-toothed speculums full
of indelible ink—retail kraken!—the sallow
       fluorescence of the middle class.

Donna C. at layaway, Pietà of summer dresses
       in her arms, yellow-belted seersucker,
fuchsia wraparound, shirred waist. I adorned
       myself for $14.99 of my father's cash,
bought a pack of jellybeans at the checkout.
       Pink plastic wedges were never a good idea.

# (ORBITALS)

Neither positive nor negative, just probabilities in a cloud. Radical love. Particles found in volumes that take several shapes—pear, donut, dumbbell. Underwire and enhanced, lace and sateen. The exact position of the particle is unknown, or rather, as soon as it is known, the position has changed, or observing the position changes it. One hand reaching for another hand. It's not a pocket, not a cave, but a mathematical function that describes its hole-like behavior. Sharp, principal, diffuse, fundamental. A lobe, a tongue. A zone of likelihood. Zone of unknowing. This one is a torus: a drum membrane, with a central antinode, a waterbed with its waves and wakes. Nothing is unclean. When you see her hesitate at the concession stand, touch her. When you see him struggle to fold the cafeteria table, touch him. Offer a hand up the back of the bleachers, an arm over the ice, a napkin to the lips: touch.

## OUR LADY OF THE PROM

In the bridal shop on Defense Highway in Marley,
        the matrons spoke of sheaths without swords,
repeat areas of lace yardage, *flounce* as a noun.
        We found our way back to the sale rack, spun
the size 8s for something to alter or slit, tea-length
        taffetas with terrible bows we could rip off
with our teeth. We were raised on cataclysm,

        outside the Beltway but too close to DC
for duck and cover, no drills for vaporization
        while we waited for the sky to flash white
over the Capitol—black box, trigger, DEFCON, dawn—

        so no one was surprised sex could kill you.
We had half of half-knowledge, knew nothing
        of calla lilies or bullwhips, alpha interferon
or ACT UP or Haring, only Mr. MacLeish choking up
        in comp explaining that *obscene* came from
keeping sex and anguish offstage—*a microphone
        shoved in a widow's face is obscene*—knew
directions to a testing place in Towson where you
        got a number and didn't have to tell them
your name. Wait six weeks. Mapplethorpe died

        in March but what did we know while we
maneuvered through First Ladies at the Smithsonian:
        ghosts of peach faille, ivory silk twill,
copper shantung. We were dreaming of simulacra
        in polyester nylon, practicing our up-dos and
feathering the front, giggling when the ladies talked
        about boning, when they spoke of La Sirène
in cream silk crepe, its exquisite fishtail, or the spokes
        of a dress made to mimic the mechanism of
an umbrella, or the 1955 butterfly—brown chiffon
        cut to convey a ruptured chrysalis and wings.

## (DEMONS)

Stand next to me, I'll take away your fears, smother them like ticks with Vaseline until they come to the surface. Your fear of snakes, theater fires, paralysis, bullies, blood cancer. Your urge to shoplift, Tetris binges, dread of embarrassment. Your worry that the universe thought you were too chicken for either a baby or an abortion. Your panic about cake, your party trick of taking a bite to chew for a while then finding a trash can to spit it in. Give me your overtired thrashing. Give me your habit of picking your face until it scabs. Give me the ache in your jaw from clenching it at night, half awake and jostled in your visions of rain-soaked crowds, searching for safety but thinking the arm in every coat's a gun. Forgive yourself for wanting to push that limping boy off the ledge at Niagara. For the equations you wrote on the inside of your wrist. For letting the lie get told until you believed it. The venom's on the tongue.

# OUR LADY OF THE SLOTS

He picked me up at seven and we drove north
        for hours. I fell asleep somewhere along
the New Jersey Turnpike and when I woke
        I didn't know where we were, Connecticut
maybe, deep seatbelt crease on my cheek.

        The place was quieter than I expected,
daylight clean. He ran his hand along the machines—
        triple cherry, triple lemon, triple bar,
nodded at the only patron in the row as torrents
        of nickels poured into her Big Gulp cup,
rolled onto the chrysanthemum carpet. He took

        off his jacket, draped it over my bare
shoulders before I knew I was cold, sat down
        at blackjack. Freddy—said the dealer's
tag—fanned the deck, flicked a lock from
        his brow, dealt another face card onto
the felt. Callahan kept winning. Winning and
        winning and winning. An acre away,

on the burlesque stage, a woman, not young,
        went through the motions with the pole.
Two guys in dark suits, razor-burned faces,
        approached and said something about
"guest services." I could see it in his face—
        his profane cognition, his ace of spades.
Maren, go get me a vodka tonic. I set off

        into the techno-bass, taffy off-gasses
and chrome. In faux woodgrain, in crumpled
        cocktail napkins, in the bulletproof window
at the cashier—the worn face of Donna Callahan.
        Before I found my way back to the table,

he grabbed my wrist, pulled me past restrooms
        and down a corridor piled with packing
crates and out an emergency exit into the night.

# (BEATITUDES)

The two Tanyas who live down the street are lucky. The hot-lunch lady is lucky. The girl who gives up her answers in homeroom is lucky. Kit-Kats are lucky. The crossing guard's raincoat is lucky. The classified jobs your mom and dad have at NSA are lucky. The stoners in detention are lucky. The fire drill during the test is lucky. The layoff is lucky. The layup is lucky. The spotter for the gymnastics team is lucky. The retainer in the dumpster is lucky. The vice principal's Pontiac is lucky. Mixing together all the different fountain sodas at 7-Eleven and calling the concoction "suicide" is not lucky. Stop doing that. The quiet man pushing the floor buffer at Kmart is lucky. Blessed are the drive-thrus. Blessed are cigarette breaks in walk-in freezers. Blessed are the loves that begin in Friendly's parking lots after hours. The geeks will inherit the earth.

## OUR LADY OF THE PERMANENT SUB

Then Heingartner quit, or got fired, no one knew.
        We'd all had him, some of us twice, for
Algebra II/Trig or Applied Math. Greg reported
        that on Monday Heingartner was mumbling
about Fibonacci and factorials and then Tuesday

        all his stuff was off the walls—equation
cartoons, Groucho Marx poster (*Outside of
        a dog, a book is a man's best friend;
inside of a dog, it's too dark to read*), his yellowed
        counted-cross-stitch sampler: *Simplify.*

The sub had fake eyelashes and a coffee mug
        that said *Juan in a million.* She told them
to copy last year's test, talked about the zodiac.

## PARABLE OF THE KEG

Keith snuck out the night before the SATs
to go to a party behind Rob Rooney's grand-
father's barn. He leaned near towers of green

pint containers, sipped bitter foam from a cup.
Someone built a bonfire and he stood back from
the blaze, the crunch of dried-up strawberry vines

underfoot, the stakes of irrigation lines snagging
his cuffs. Panicked about the time, he accepted
a ride in the cold open bed of a pickup truck.

# OUR LADY OF THE AUDITORIUM

Rumor had it Heingartner had been run out
      of town. We were nervous—we suspected
Callahan knew more than he let on, and he was
      visibly upset. That Friday was the dumb
variety show but no one wanted to go back
      to school for it, except for Oscar who
had to be there on account of his sister's solo,
      his mother had made that much clear.

When Oscar got back, he was out of breath,
      gesturing while we tried to sort out
his garble of *principal* and *lip sync* and *leotard*.
      He said Dawn Drake's mother made
Principal Byers do it—made Byers fire him.

      Everyone knew Byers was having an affair
with Dawn Drake's mother, so we figured
      she hated Heingartner for some reason
and got him fired. Then Oscar reported how
      after intermission Dawn Drake danced
the Mr. Macavity number from *Cats* with
      audible purrs, and the boys and Byers
in the front row crossed their legs over their
      boners and their arms over their disgrace.

## GARAGE GOSPEL

I got slut-shamed by the lacrosse team once I started being seen

with Callahan around town. Pizza Hut two-for-one deep dish on
    Thursday nights. Sitting on the same side of the table with Parker
    between us—he reached his arm over the back of the booth to
    stroke my ear.

*Loose,* they hooted, holding their placemats in front of their faces like
    daily papers.

Callahan got up and wiped his mouth, told us to meet him on the
    baseball diamond at the middle school in an hour,

then didn't show.

We scrambled the cash for the pizza and ran over there, but he didn't
    come.

We waited.

We waited and I worried.

I worried his car broke down, his mom got sick, his heart stopped, his
    dad showed up, his ex showed up, he left the stove on, he left me,
    he left town,

crossed my arms over my chest, tugged the hem of my culottes a little
    lower while the boys

stood around scuffing up dirt in sulfur-rose clouds,

vaporous, if vapor could be dry,

trading insults in the waxing fear as it got too dark to see.

This is stupid, Jordan Cisco said.

No one answered him so he said to Zack, And we don't even know—
   what *is* he?

and Zack said, What is he what? What *what*?

I thought about Callahan's sleek curls on his neck, dampening as he
   slept,

about his body, his black lashes and the shape of his skull.

Levi kept looking at his watch.

We waited.

Then without a sound Callahan appeared

*and all the people gathered round him.*

Conditioned to the classroom, we sat in the grass along the foul line.

The waiting evaporated into moonlight.

*He had taken his seat and was engaged in teaching them when the scribes
   and the Pharisees brought in a woman caught committing adultery.*

Then some of the lacrosse players showed up,

emerging from the trees on the bleacher side, a cackling pack of
   them, pointing—that's the nerd who sleeps with teachers.

*Making her stand in the middle, they said to him,*

*"Teacher, this woman was caught in the very act of adultery. In the law
   Moses has laid down that such women are to be stoned. What do you
   say about it?"*

*They put the question as a test, hoping to frame a charge against him. He
bent down and wrote with his finger on the ground.*

*When they continued to press their question he sat up straight and said, "Let
whichever of you is free from sin throw the first stone at her." Then once
again he bent down and wrote on the ground.*

*When they heard what he said, one by one they went away, the eldest first;
and he was left alone, with the woman standing there.*

He sat back.

*"Where are they? Nobody has condemned you?"*

Nobody, I said.

I don't either, he said.

## PARABLE OF THE DONUT

Sean never stole anything before, but as he cut
through the backyard on his way to the woods
he saw the screen door open and could hear

the shower running. The purse was sitting right
there on the counter, an uncapped ballpoint pen
sticking out of the pocket. He scrawled WACH

OUT on the wall, ran, found his friends eating
stale donuts in a lean-to they made with a few
pieces of lumber and rotting drywall against

a boulder, one of several excavated and dumped
at the edge of the development when foundations
were dug. He counted the cash, less than $20,

stashed a sunken jelly donut into the purse
and threw it across the dirt bike trail. When
the police returned it to her, it was full of ants.

# (MIRACLES)

When it turned out all it was was a mangled spoon tucked into the garbage disposal. The hour the antibiotics kicked in. The last outbound train running ten minutes late. Your aunt hitting the lotto in time to make the mortgage. The thick envelope. The light left on in the van but the engine still turning over. *The proximity of the neighbor.* The expired meter with no ticket. The time when you hesitated, and she took your hand. When you coughed, but he was looking at something else. When you ran out of gas, and he helped you push the car into the parking space at Casa Real. The key to the library bathroom. The rusted padlock. The handkerchief in the pocket. The extension cord. The tarp in the trunk. The single dry match. Stand clear of the closing doors.

## OUR LADY OF KENTUCKY FRIED CHICKEN

It was raining, so Mrs. C. pulled all the way
        down the driveway and handed Callahan
the bags of food through the window. He ducked
        under the half-open garage door and Parker

went to slam it down but Callahan stopped him:
        *pace,* friend, let's let in some air. Someone
needed a shower, or a sandwich had gotten kicked
        under the couch, or a mouse had died.
Mrs. C. backed out with her arm thrown over
        the seat, checking mirrors. Zack told

a joke about an Irish husband and a battery.
        Oscar fiddled with the frayed cord
of the amp, juiced himself a little. Danny said,
        I'm nervous about this, would somebody
listen, for God's sake? Levi stared out at the rain
        and the half streetscape visible under
the door, leaning forward until a UPS truck
        across the street rumbled to life again
and pulled away. I peeled my nails, watched

        Callahan's breaths settle on our shoulders.
*He looked around with anger and sorrow at their*
        *obstinate stupidity,* started pulling supper
out of the bags: Original and Extra Crispy,
        mashed potatoes and gravy in equal tubs,
biscuits with packets of butter and grape jelly.
        Last he plunked down two two-liters:
one Sprite, one Coke. Tossed me a cup.

*Take this, he said, and drink from it, this is*
the last one. No one talked, just ate. Then Levi
      said he heard that Heingartner was under
house arrest in Pennsylvania, brought up on
      federal charges for having child porn
in his darkroom. Parker slammed the door down
      so hard it bounced a few inches then settled
on its chain. Callahan knew. He looked at me,

      eyes dimmed. He knew Jordan Cisco
would wipe his lips on a napkin, flex. He knew
      he was going out to talk to the press.

# OUR LADY OF FORMICA

We didn't know what to do so we went to Mrs. C.—
      Parker, Levi, and I—knocked on the door
of her yellow bungalow behind the A&P. No answer.
      We pounded again, waited, and she appeared
in a chenille bathrobe, blue bandana over her perm.

      She sat us down at her dinette, passed a bowl
of grapes. I'm going to tell you everything I know,
      she said. He loves you, and he doesn't want
to see anyone get hurt. Jordan Cisco told the police

      Callahan had molested his sister, a junior
on the pep squad, and she had given a statement.
      Jordan said he was surprised to find Callahan
in the woodshop when he went to get his sister
      after she picked up her wood-burning project,
a gift for their mother: *leave room in your garden*
      *for the angels to dance.* Along the side table
there were rows of molded key chains the freshmen
      were making, bubbles hardened in. When he

walked in, Jordan said, Callahan was standing behind
      her and pressing his hips into hers. The smell
of plastic resin made him sick. He noticed that someone
      had drawn a penis on the seat for the jigsaw
but conceded that it was probably already there. He saw
      Mr. Callahan's hand on her thigh. For the rest
of the testimony, he said, you'd have to ask her.

## DENIAL

The reporter caught Parker off guard.

*He followed him at a distance, to see how it would all end.*

He had been crying and he wiped his nose with his sleeve.

Did he know this science teacher, this Mr. Callahan? Had he taken
any classes with him? What did he think about this string of
shocking allegations in his hometown? Not one but two young
male teachers accused of sex abuse—was it true they were
cousins? What did he think was the nature of their relationship?

Parker flinched, looked away,

"He was always, um, you know, a little off."

# DISPASSION (FRIDAY)

The weather was a factor. By six the story was all over
the local news in ten-minute loops—Gambrills man

brought up on harassment and assault charges, James
Callahan, Jr., science teacher at Kinneret High School,

indicted on four counts of—Parker slammed off the TV.
The garage was cold but I didn't feel cold. To say there was

a thunderstorm is an understatement—turbid green sky,
golf-ball hail, Jake howling Auntie Em! Auntie Em!

Parker had been sulking and raging all afternoon, Zack
at his side, muttering, Where is he? Where the hell is he?

Did he say anything to you before he left the gym? Why
don't you go home for a while, Parker, you're—It's not

the Mountain Dew, Oscar said, and Parker slammed
his fist into the wall, next to the last hole he punched

in the wall, screamed Motherfucker! and went out.
I can see every one of their faces as plain as I see yours

right now. It was dark around seven. Someone had switched
on *Family Feud.* I didn't hear a car door or any door,

but suddenly Callahan was there, standing on the lion stain,
asking where Parker was. He had on jeans and a phys ed

department sweatshirt stenciled "Medium." I tried to
touch him, stroked then tugged his arm, but he shook off

my hand. Parker said he would be right back, Zack said.
The weather was a factor. There was never any other time

in our lives, not before, not since, when we wanted anyone
to stay with us as much as we wanted him to stay with us

that night. Callahan put his fingers to his temples, paced.
Zack kept talking to himself, trying to make sense of it—

Was it a charge of subversion? Was it time to plot the coup?
Did he want us to get the marching band involved?

Jake came in soaking wet, said to Callahan, You have to
get down there. Where, where? Zack said. Get where?

Callahan looked around wildly, then straight at me.
His eyes filled. *All she asks's the strength to hold me.*

And he was gone. I remember worrying I'd throw up.
Oscar went for keys, came back, and I got in with Jake

and Danny in his mom's van, his baby sister's booster seat
between us. I don't know how we knew where to go but

we did—Wolf Pit Road, the long straightaway where
they taught us to do U-turns in driver's ed. The hail

along the side of the road had blown in clusters like
Styrofoam peanuts. The weather was a factor. Later,

not then, we heard about the police car on the dead end
turning on its lights. Later, not then, we heard about

Callahan carrying the textbooks in milk crates, slipping
on the loading dock. Later, not then, we heard about

how he sped out the high school driveway onto Rte. 175
trying to catch Parker before he got to the quarry. A half

mile later, the Nissan had flipped over the guardrail and
rolled down the embankment into a stand of trees.

# (WRECK)

*Can I go on with this train of events?* I know what you saw, and I knew you would see it, and I am sorry. Mangled hood like the head of a dragon. Flipped turtle, crumpled pie pan, crowbar, skull. Shattered glass, a door ripped off the chassis. No one knows the force that pried back that door, the fragile tenacity of soft tissue and bone, its reluctance to give way. Blunt trauma to the spleen, concussed cerebrum— gray and white against the battered cloud mass along the western horizon. *Watching the reel brutally taking its time.* They'll threaten suspension, expulsion, call it the delusions of a pervert or pothead, call it counterfeit and un-American, an alchemist's apocrypha, a fool tuned in to transformation on the FM dial. So be it. Listen to me, Maren, listen to me. Wreck to the left, wreck to the right, the good thief and the bandit. Brown out, then black out, then total dark.

# DISPASSION (SATURDAY)

We met at the dead mall in Marley—Mike T. broke in
behind the receiving dock and we climbed from wall to wall

on planters, through browned fronds of ornamental palms,
through storefront gates half pulled down, plate glass pocked

with spiderweb shatters—not bullets, just stones. Parker
stood on the edge of the dried-up fountain, kicked aqua

nuggets of glass: *here lie the ghosts of Black Friday, here rise retail
spirits from sarcophagi.* Shut the hell up, Levi said, led the ten

down the defunct escalator, the ten and Rachelle and Kim
and me, and Jake's sister, one by one through the dust of

texturized plaster, over ripped-out track lighting, around
the curtainless photo booths. We smoked on the mezzanine

above the kites and kiosks, all the trademarks scrubbed off,
the signs pulled down except Amira's Pretzel Hut and Claire's.

We gathered on the carpeted tiers of the Santa amphitheater—
Gap Zales Häagen-Dazs Bombay—tossing crusted pennies

down the shaft of a glass elevator before ducking out an exit
and dispersing across the empty parking lot by twos and threes

while the rest of us huddled under the white canyon walls
of department stores, windowless, four stories high.

# DISPASSION (SUNDAY)

If I went out the front I'd wake my parents with the click
of the deadbolt so I lifted the guest room sash and tumbled

into the forsythia and out. I got pollen on my hands, wiped
them on my jeans. *I do not know where they have laid him.* Full

moon beside the silo. I walked along the drainage ditch,
careful to stay outside the rumble strip, though there were

no cars at that hour. I scanned the shoulder for skid marks,
for the tamped-down patch of underbrush, until I saw

the wreck of a gray car almost invisible in the trees. *With
these words she turned round and saw him standing there but she did*

*not recognize him, thinking it was* a state trooper. His body
blocked the moon, his waist slim as a girl's. He was

barefoot among the skunk cabbages with a sock tan, a rip
in his flank revealing a sheath of fat, beside the wreck

of a gray car, its door pried *up,* hinge dangling. I saw his
ripped jersey, smelled his ripe sweat. He spoke. *Go tell*

*Parker and the others you saw me but don't tell anyone else, okay?*
*Okay? Maren?* There was sticky blood on his face, a blue

tint in the sky. I reached out to try to touch his face.
*Let go. Let go of me. Let go of me. Let go of me. Let go of me.*

## OUR LADY OF THE PRICKER BUSH

The boy was startled to find me there, crouching
      behind the garage, my head on my knees,
grabs of grass in my hands. His face was bathed
      in dread, or mine was—I didn't know who
had gotten to him or what he knew, knew only my
      terror and the pebbles pressed in my knees
as I fell forward onto the slate under the woodpile,
      bull thistle pricking my arms. I asked him

who he was, then figured it out—he was Matt,
      the drummer they found to replace Jordan.
A sophomore the size of a sixth grader, ginger,
      freckled, more than one wart on his thumb,
he sat down next to me and I pressed my hand over
      his hand, five fingers spread over five, my
touch a balm and a warning, press of succor, shock.

## GARAGE GOSPEL

I lifted the heavy door without knocking, felt the bass before I heard it.

Parker said, You scared the shit out of me.

It's just Maren, someone said.

*I will teach you about what is hidden from you.*

Parker lobbed an empty can, said, I can't deal with you right now.

I shook my head, put up my hand,

*I will teach you about what is hidden from you.*

Here. Here's the account I set down. I wrote it out on a legal pad the
    same night and put it in a manila envelope with a wing clasp,
    and I took it in a box with my important papers for half a dozen
    moves. It's not all there anymore—the box was in a leaky attic
    at one point and I don't know, who needs these things. I guess I
    didn't throw it out because I didn't throw it out.

*This why you get si[c]k and die: because [you love] what de[c]ei[ve]s [you].*

*(Pages 1–6 are missing.)*

They didn't want to listen to me but I grabbed the bag of chips away
    from Parker with such crinkly ferocity they shut up.

The slash between us and them is nothing, I said.

I said, We need to dissolve it, like Callahan said. *Love is strong as death.*

Parker mocked me with a pelvic thrust. Tell me, how *did* we get
    naughty from naught? How's your nothing?

*Will m[a]tter then be utterly [destr]oyed or not?*

Levi tried to get around the table.

*Sister, we know that the Savior loved you more than all other women. Tell us the words of the Savior that you remember, the things which you know that we don't because we haven't heard them.*

Parker shoved Levi's arm away.

Parker said, *Did he speak with a woman in private without us knowing about it? Are we to turn around and listen to her?*

Levi grabbed his arm.

I felt bile in my throat, and a tilt inside my head, like the floor had slid off a pallet.

*I am who I am / and what I am / is what I am / are what you are / or what?*

*She turned their heart [to]ward the Good and they began to deba[t]e about the wor[d]s of [the Savior].*

*Say my name / Sun shines through the rain / A whole life so lonely / And then you come and ease the pain*

Parker said, With a body like that who needs college.

I kept talking.

*I saw the Lord in a vision today and I said to him, "Lord, I saw you today in a vision."*

My eyes moved to where a piece of ivy had grown between the cinderblock and wood frame near the door. Parker reached down and ripped it out.

*When the soul had brought the third Power to naught.*

To naught.

Too naughty.

*[Ma]tter gav[e bi]rth to a passion which has no Image because it derives from what is contrary to nature. A disturbing confusion then occurred in the whole body.*

Levi stood up and Parker backed him hard against the unpainted drywall. Nail heads weathered into relief.

I spoke louder. I spoke as fast as I could.

*And Desire said, I did not see you go down, yet now I see you go up. So why do you lie since you belong to me?*

Parker laughed, What's the difference?

To naught.

*The seven powers of wrath: darkness, desire, ignorance, zeal for death, realm of the flesh, foolish wisdom of the flesh, wisdom of wrath.*

Oscar picked up a piece of chalk and wrote on the floor:

human = killer = space = conqueror

*sees the vision an[d] that is w[hat]*

Someone said, Turn up the TV I can't hear with this bullshit going on!

*We should clothe ourselves with the perfect human.*

*I saw him in a vision and I said to him, "I saw you today in a vision." He answered me, "How wonderful you are for not wavering at seeing me! For where the mind is, there is the treasure."*

Oscar said, The motherfucker was a materialist marionette.

*You [mis]took the garment [I wore] for my [true] self.*

*(Pages 11–14 are missing.)*

I sat down

*wept matter utterly topic promulgate wavering wept naught zeal killer*
    *choose private wept ashamed preach disobedient root choose wept*

Someone said, I have no idea what she is talking about.

*Do you think that I have thought up these things by myself in my heart or*
    *that I am telling lies about the Savior?*

For where the mind is, there is the treasure.

*Did he, then, speak with a woman in private without our knowing about it?*
    *Are we to turn around and listen to her? Did he choose her over us?*

Levi got up and shoved him.

*wept*

Levi stuck up for me against Parker.

Levi stuck up for me.

# (TONGUES)

Get out of the county before graduation. It's a waste of your time and you'll roast in the heat, and nobody will listen to you anyway. You can't stay in this sweltering cenacle, this rancid garage. No one needs to stick around to find out if they open a Subway. Danny, go to Florida. Greg, you get Texas. Lorenzo, take the Pacific Northwest. Jeff, go to Ohio. Zack, go to Maine. Mike T., SoCal, but stay away from Venice Beach. Oscar, head somewhere in the Upper Midwest. Lakes and ice. The rest of you, spread out along the seaboards. When you want fresh breath, cinnamon: Big Red, Mike and Ikes, Red Hots, Atomic Fireballs. When you get to a new place, watch the live footage, the security cams. Pay attention to their additives, their sideburns—*your young men will see visions and your old men will dream dreams.* Watch every episode of *America's Most Wanted. Part the crowd.* Keep right. Once in a while, eat a vegetable. Stack their shopping carts, loosen the locked wheels, steer their school buses, staple their receipts. Listen to their litigation and their rumors, their knock-knock jokes, committee minutes, euphemisms, campaign slogans, press releases, haiku, complaints. *Enter by the narrow gate.*

## (SCRIPT)

*Your accuser is Moses. No bullying, no blackmail. Are you discussing that saying of mine: a little while and you will not see me, and again in a little while, you will not see me? Send him to dip the tip of his finger in water, to cool my tongue. Lip service. When the river was in flood, it burst upon that house. If you say so, I will let down the nets. Till now I have been using figures of speech: a time is coming when I shall no longer use figures, but tell you in plain words. My flesh is real food. Does this shock you? I have come to set fire to the earth, and how I wish it were already kindled. There will be a stench. Stop, no more of that. Peace is my parting gift.*

# (ASCENSION)

Go down to Jiffy Lube in the middle of the week and wait for the guy to push himself out from under a car on a dolly. He will sit up and wipe his hands on a towel. Ask for antifreeze and wiper blades. Tell him: *a railroad runs through the record stores at night.* When someone asks where I went, tell them: *he fastened his coat around him, for he had stripped, and plunged into the sea.* As for the rest     *this rabble rebuked the wind and sea*     change machines     *pigeons mixture of myrrh and     pretext where the carcass     tethered colt     no more of that!     tried to seize     already kindled behind locked doors     raiment     privily     axe to the root palsy     publicans     mote     if he ask a fish*

# OUR LADY OF FRANK'S NURSERY & CRAFTS

I wasn't going to read from his script,
  let alone Parker's. Before he disappeared
the last time, I left town, took Amtrak to Atlanta
  to stay with my aunt, started school again
down there. *Everyone will be salted with fire.*

  My kids keep me busy. The man I married
is a good man, a reliable lover, preoccupied
  with his work. He leaves me time to think,
to make my wreaths—I grow and cut flowers,
  lay them in bins filled with silica gel.
Roses do well, but I've never liked the smell,
  too much like my grandmother's soap,
scent of the pre-corpse. I like Russian sage and
  helichrysum, salvia and love-in-a-mist,
sometimes sea lavender. I couldn't stay there.

  If I stayed he would have made me
one of his ghosts. Not that any of us escaped
  without damage, cinematic dreams.
You tuck the end in and secure it with binding
  wire, then wrap it with matte green tape
for camouflage, twist. It's not rocket science.
  Delphinium, if you support the stalk.

In the dreams, I go looking for him in intricate
  urban darkness, transit grids, overlays
of places I've been: Quito, Rochester, New Orleans.
  When I find him, there are purulent gaps
in his gums, a slit in his side. I've learned how
  to wake myself—swim to the surface—
get up, do some housekeeping, head out
  as soon as the stores open, for supplies—
straight pins, copper wire, rings. Green blocks
  of foam remind me oddly of food, confection.

I like it there, among the gnomes and hoses,
    squirrel-proof feeders and bags of mulch.

I look over sometimes and see Donna Callahan
    waiting for the staff to open another register.

## RENUNCIATION (HALF LIFE)

Each year my faith decays by half, then half again.
   In this way it is infinite. What use is bitterness?
That would be like trying to seed the clouds to divert

  a hurricane, dissolve it at sea. He follows me
everywhere and I talk to him inside my head,
   intercellular and atmospheric, within and with-
out, spliced into my genes and dotting the radar.
   I don't know, Barbara, am I making sense?
Are you getting all this down? All I know is he was

  dead, mangled in a wreck, and then he was back,
angling his tongue into my mouth in his urgent way.
   *Other signs not recorded in this book.* Sightings.

We loved him, and love can make you see crazy things.
   Off the record, ok? You sure you have that thing
turned off? Maybe we missed him so hard our anguish

  took the shape of him. A vision, a hallucination—
something like that. Or maybe not, maybe he cheated death
   and gathered his electrons into the unknowable

spaces of their lack, set them moving in radiant orbitals
   we sense only in their harmonics, in the shadow
of their severance. Does it matter? Either way, I'm just

  sitting here with you at this table. Either way he's
gone. The abyss, the gulf between us—what is that line?
   Bade between us be? *The unplumb'd, salt, estranging sea.*

# NOTES

The first and third *Garage Gospels* interweave quotations from the apocryphal Gospel of Mary, a fragmentary book discovered in 1896 in a fifth-century papyrus codex. Believed to have been written in Greek in the second century, it is often interpreted as a Gnostic text. Whether or not it recounts the words and actions of Mary of Magdala during the lifetime of Jesus of Nazareth remains in question, though many believe that no other Mary could play the roles described—witness of the Resurrection, companion of Jesus, leader among the disciples, and interpreter of Jesus' ministry. The Mary of this account establishes the authority of women to carry revelation.

Other scriptural fragments throughout, most in italics, refer to the New Testament gospels in their translations in *The Oxford Study Bible: Revised English Bible with the Apocrypha,* edited by M. Jack Suggs, Katharine Doob Sakenfeld, and James R. Mueller, though occasionally passages from other biblical translations are used.

*(Teacher)* invokes Sonic Youth's 1988 album *Daydream Nation* and ends with a line from Depeche Mode, "Personal Jesus" (1989).

*(Kiddie Pool)* echoes the line "the insurgency began and you missed it" from R.E.M., "Begin the Begin" (1986).

*(Homeopath)* includes the line "let's put our heads together and start a new country up" from R.E.M., "Cuyahoga" (1986).

*Our Lady of 80s Punk* incorporates and alters bits of lyrics from Sonic Youth, "Teen Age Riot" (1986); The Replacements, "Bastards of Young" (1985); and Joy Division, "Disorder" (1979).

*(Half Life)* includes the line "I'm your messiah and you're the reason why" from Prince, "I Will Die 4 U" (1984).

*Our Lady of the Access Road* draws color from Gerhard Richter, *10.8.89 [Betty]* 1989, oil on color photograph.

*Our Lady of the Quarry* includes the lines "sitting in a sand pit, life is a short trip, the music's for the sad man" from Alphaville, "Forever Young" (1984).

The final lines of *Our Lady of the Prom* draw inspiration from *Charles James: Beyond Fashion*, The Metropolitan Museum of Art, 2014.

The italicized line in *(Miracles)* quotes Emmanuel Levinas, "Peace and Proximity."

In *Dispassion (Friday)*, "All she asks's the strength to hold me" is from Joy Division, "Ceremony" (1981).

The italicized lines in *(Wreck)* are from Joy Division, "Passover" (1980).

Some imagery in *Dispassion (Saturday)* is indebted to Seph Lawless's photographs of the abandoned Rolling Acres Mall in Akron, Ohio.

The third *Garage Gospel* regrafts a line from Edie Brickell & New Bohemians, "What I Am" (1988) with its sources in Exodus 3:14 and 1 Corinthians 15:10, and echoes lines from The Bangles, "Eternal Flame" (1988).

The first italicized sentence in *(Ascension)* is from Sonic Youth, "Eric's Trip" (1988). The rest of the fragments are scripture.

*Renunciation (Half Life)* owes a turn of phrase and thought to Timothy Donnelly and his mom, and ends with the final line of Matthew Arnold's "To Marguerite: Continued."

Any resemblance Maren bears to Magdalena in payroll in The Roches' "Jesus Shaves" (2007), though not unwelcome, is entirely coincidental.

# ACKNOWLEDGMENTS

With thanks to the editors of *Poetry International* and *Blue Earth Review* for publishing portions of this story.

I'm grateful to Jennifer Franklin, Simon Waxman, and Stefania Heim for reading drafts and offering counsel at the inflection points, to Bill Waddell for bringing the music, and to Kathy Fagan for her faith in the thing. And always and beyond measure to John.